Read & Respond

Read & Respond

FOR
KS2

Author: Huw Thomas

Development Editor: Simret Brar

Editor: Dodi Beardshaw

Assistant Editor: Francis Ridley

Series Designer: Anna Oliwa

Designers: Mohammed Iqbal Aslam / Sonja Bagley

Illustrations: Jane Bottomley

Text © 2008, Huw Thomas © 2008, Scholastic Ltd

Designed using Adobe InDesign

Published by Scholastic Ltd,
Book End, Range Road, Witney,
Oxfordshire OX29 0YD

www.scholastic.co.uk

Printed by Bell & Bain

9   6 7

British Library Cataloguing-in-Publication Data
A catalogue record for this book is available from the British
Library.

ISBN 978-1407-10041-8

Acknowledgements
The publishers gratefully acknowledge permission to reproduce
the following copyright material: **United Artists** for the use
of extracts from *Stormbreaker* by Anthony Horowitz © 2000,
Anthony Horowitz (2000, Walker Books).

Stormbreaker

About the book

Stormbreaker is a classic secret agent story – but with a difference. The secret agent is a fourteen-year-old. When his guardian and uncle is mysteriously killed, teenager Alex Rider finds himself recruited by MI6 and sent to work undercover on the job that killed his secret agent uncle.

The resultant adventure moves from London, to an SAS training camp, then on to Cornwall and back to the capital.

About the author

Anthony Horowitz was 'thick at school', to quote his words in a newspaper interview. The author, who has gone on to write best-selling books and television programmes, spent his teenage years at the bottom of the class, bullied and overweight. He now finds himself the author of over 50 books that have sold across the world, and been adapted for film. These include the television series 'Foyle's War' and, of course, the Alex Rider stories about the youngest secret agent in MI6.

Anthony was born in 1956, in Middlesex. He has been writing stories since the age of eight and has been a professional author since he was 20. He can spend up to ten hours a day writing in a specially comfortable shed in his garden, equipped with a bedroom for the times when he writes too late into the night.

There was a fair bit of secrecy in Anthony's childhood. His father, a wealthy businessman, was someone Anthony describes as a 'fixer' for Harold Wilson, the former Prime Minister.

Anthony was sent to boarding school at the age of eight and found himself in a horror of an establishment, run by a headteacher who flogged boys till they bled. However, as a child he loved the escapism of James Bond films. These were part of the inspiration for Alex Rider. Recalling his childhood, Anthony says the Alex stories are fuelled by memories of his own teenage dreams, recalling the things he would have liked to have done and the hero he would have liked to have been. Yet, in writing the stories, he puts himself through many of the things Alex Rider faces. For Stormbreaker he put himself through SAS training, climbed up onto the roof of the Science museum in London and experienced what it's like to remain up to the last minute in a car that is being crushed in a breaker's yard. He also gets his son to try some of the Alex Rider thrills, like diving and snowboarding. That must be so cool!

Alongside the Alex Rider books, Anthony is producing the *Power of Five* series, a set of five horror stories. He has also written some daring horror stories, which are so chilling they rouse a bit of controversy. He also wrote the story *Granny*, drawing on his own experience of having a Grandmother whom he hated – he and his sister danced on her grave after she died.

Alongside *Stormbreaker* the Alex Rider stories continue with *Point Blanc*, *Skeleton Key*, *Eagle Strike*, *Scorpia*, *Ark Angel* and *Snakehead*, making up a truly thrilling library of secret agent adventure.

> **Facts and figures**
> *Stormbreaker*
> First published by Walker books 2000
> Shorlisted for the Children's Books Award 2001

Guided reading

Introducing the book

Begin by asking children about the genre of secret agent and action stories, either in films or fiction. List some of the better known titles. What sort of features do these stories have in common? Make connections between the goodies and baddies in the various stories and the different ways in which problems are solved and hazards are tackled.

This is the point at which you need to tackle the fact that some of the group may already be familiar with *Stormbreaker*, by pointing out that if they have seen the film they can relive it through the book. For those who have listened to it on tape or read it at home, point out that reading in a group will help them to explore the story, but ask them to do their best not to provide 'plot-spoilers' at every reading.

Look at the blurb on the back of the book. Ask the children to find the particular sentences that would most make them want to read the book – either in the blurb or a press notice.

Chapters 1 to 3

Start by asking children to read through Chapter 1. It starts with tragedy, but there's little grieving as the puzzles begin straight away. Ask the children to look through the chapter and take note of all the suspicious moments in these early stages.

Ask the children to read to the end of Chapter 2, the scene in the junk yard. What sort of scenes does this remind them of in other action stories they have read or seen? Consider how well devised the danger is – how horrible. Ask them to look through the scene where Alex realises he in trouble and find the lines that communicate the sense of danger and entrapment.

Reading to the end of Chapter 3, ask the children why they think Alex behaves the way he does when asked to visit the bank. He is suspicious by now. Why do the children think this is the case? This is a good point to consider what is going on in the story as a whole. At this point we don't know the goodies from the baddies. What do children think of Blunt? What sort of a character is he? Direct the children to the way he watches Alex nearly fall to his death – what does this tell us about the man?

Ask the children to list the unanswered questions that still hang over the story.

Chapters 4 to 6

Ask the children to read through the conversation Alex has with Blunt in Chapter 4 and ask themselves how these two are getting on with each other. What do they think of each other?

The conversation is frosty. What creates this tension? Note the refusal to tell Alex about Ian's death and the fact that Alex initially refuses to work for MI6. What do the children think of the way in which Alex is blackmailed into working? Why do they think Alex refused? Why did Blunt resort to such measures?

Review the conversation about Herod Sayle and ask the children to imagine they were a team of secret agents. What would they think of Sayle, based purely on the evidence of this conversation? What comes across as being positive about this character? What is it that undermines the apparent generosity?

Ask the children to read the first few pages of Chapter 5. What was it like for Alex to walk into that room full of SAS trainees? Is it not possible that a story could be written where such people sympathetically warm to the little kid and adopt him as a troop mascot? Why doesn't this happen here? Home in on the sergeant's first words and the way the rest of the group talk about Alex.

Ask children to read on to the end of Chapter 6, keeping a particular eye on the character of Wolf. How does he differ from the other SAS trainees? Note the way in which, at the end of Chapter 5, the conversation with the sergeant and the incident with the matches are changing our view of Alex.

Explain to the children that the response of

a group can sometimes be represented by one character. How does Wolf serve this function? What are we told about the reactions of the others? Read the scene on the plane and the moment when he is reunited with Alex at the end of the chapter. What has happened here and why?

Chapters 7 to 10

Ask the children to think of things that give them the creeps; then ascertain that they can all imagine what a huge jellyfish looks like.

They should read through Chapter 7, imagining they are Alex, approaching Sayle enterprises. What thoughts and feelings do they think would be conjured up by first encounters with the Sayle compound, Sayle himself and Mr Grin?

Ask them to consider the different things that formed their first impression of Herod Sayle. What was the effect of the place where he is encountered – with that jellyfish tank? What about his appearance and the things he said? What did they think of the snooker game?

Having discussed these impressions, ask children to the end of Chapter 9, particularly noting the conversation Sayle has with Alex regarding security.

Having read Chapters 8 and 9, ask children to recollect the various bits of snooping around in which Alex has engaged. What has he had to do and what has he discovered? Focus on the trip to the hidden beach. What do the children think was happening that night? Direct them to the tension when a box is dropped – what does this tell us about the goings on at Sayle Enterprises?

Ask the children to read Chapter 10. They are not to take notes but when they finish the chapter they are to debrief like a group of spies, reconstructing step-by-step what took place in the long grass. Try to get details like the number of quad bikes and what happened to the riders. Once they have tried doing this amongst themselves they can check details in the book.

Chapters 11 to 13

In this section of the guided reading children will come across answers to the questions that have underpinned the mystery. Before reading, ask them to clarify what questions the book has raised and what we are waiting to find out. Ask them also to consider the clues that have been given – particularly things left by Ian Rider. What could that scribble have meant? Then ask the children to read through Chapter 11 to the point where they can answer the question about the scribble. What clues formed this trail?

Reading to the end of Chapter 11, ask the children to collate insights into what Alex is thinking and feeling. There are various ways, including his direct thoughts and the way he weighs up a dilemma, that give some insight into these.

Ask the children to skim through Chapter 11. Had they been Alex's partner, what would they have said at different points in the journey? What advice and warnings would they have given?

Before they read Chapter 12 tell the children that, if Alex gets into Sayle Enterprises, he may be discovered. What could he do in that situation? Ask them to read on through Chapter 12 and find out how Alex handles discovery by a guard and how he is eventually captured.

Chapter 13 is a classic motif in such stories – the villain reveals the plan. Once they have read this ask them to reconsider the character of Sayle. He's had a tough life – have they any sympathy for the villain?

Chapters 14 to 17

Before they continue reading ask the children to think through the potential danger offered by the jelly fish and to predict what may happen with it and how Alex might handle any encounter.

Once they have offered suggestions on this, tell the children the pace is about to accelerate and ask them to read through to the end of

Guided reading

Chapter 16.

Ask the children to skim back through Chapter 14 and find the two lines that form the most exciting moment in the chapter – is it the brush with the jellyfish or the final escape? What would they select?

Once they have read to the end of Chapter 16 ask them to draw quick and simple diagrams of the two big stunts that make up the action of the final chapters – the chasing of the plane and the scene at the Science Museum.

As they read Chapter 17 ask the children to evaluate the character of Yassen. He's a villain, but is there a hint of respect there at the end?

Take a final look across the book with the children, asking them to flick through and locate certain features, including the most exciting moment in the story - looking at what made the chosen event memorable. Was there a point where the story lulled? Some children may quote the SAS training as a diversion - it's worth revisiting any points raised as 'lulls' and seeing how they add to the story.

Finally, what were the main twists and turns in the story? At what point did things take a turn for the better in Alex's quest to complete his mission?

Shared reading

Extract 1

● Focus on the sentence that begins 'If he…' Ask the children what sort of ideas that suggests? Work out how high 70 metres is and the sort of jump involved.

● Read part of the story preceding this and check that children are clear about the nature of the scenario and the danger involved. Is Alex really having a 'stupid idea'?

● Draw a line under the words 'Do it'. Ask the children what the difference is between the paragraph before these words, and the paragraph after them. A lot of time is spent weighing up the action. What effect does this have on us as?

● Ask the children to find the argument *against* jumping, and then the argument *for* jumping. What is the factor that makes Alex decide to go ahead with the jump? (The danger is in his mind, because he is afraid of the drop.) Can the children explain Alex's move from 'thinking' to 'not thinking'?

● Alex jumps and we switch to a camera. How does the delay in knowing what happened to Alex influence the reader? Point out that switching scenes can induce suspense – a tactic children may try later when they are writing their own secret agent stories.

Extract 2

● Read the first line and ask the children what sort of insight this gives us into the character of Herod Sayle? Children may eat fish and chips but what about the words he uses – why are they disturbing?

● Read through to Alex's dredged-up facts and ask the children to pick apart the gaffe Alex has made here. Why does this work as a joke? How does it contribute to the initial relationship the agent and the villain are building up?

● Underline and re-read the two different points of view regarding the jellyfish. How do they contrast?

What kind of emotions would you feel if you only read one or the other and how does their appearing together make for an effective contrast?

● Here we have a secret agent being shown a deadly jellyfish by the villain. At this point, can the children guess what will happen somewhere later in the story? Why is it inevitable they'll end up in the same tank?

● Alex makes his near deadly mistake. What would the children have done if they were in that situation? How can Alex get out of this? And why did he make the mistake in the first place?

Extract 3

● What sort of dangers is Alex facing if he swims through a freezing, underground tunnel? Read through the first paragraph and list the ways this could go wrong.

● Throughout the book readers need to be reminded that this is not fun. Why might this be necessary? Do the children think there are times when Alex's life might come across as good fun? When and why might this be?

● At what point does Alex change and become resolved to swim the tunnel? What changes him?

● How does the description of the wet suit contribute to the feelings in this section? We've moved from excitement to fear and misery. How does the passage build up that feeling?

● Compare this passage with the first shared read. Is there a difference in the speed and attitude with which Alex embraces danger in one and not in the other? Why might this be?

Extract 1

From Chapter 3

The flag fluttered again and, seeing it, Alex went over to the window. The pole jutted out of the building exactly halfway between rooms 1504 and 1505. If he could somehow reach it, he should be able to jump on to the ledge that ran along the side of the building outside room 1504. Of course, he was fifteen floors up. If he jumped and missed there would be about seventy metres to fall. It was a stupid idea. It wasn't even worth thinking about.

Alex opened the window and climbed out. It was better not to think about it at all. He would just do it. After all, if this had been the ground floor, or a climbing-frame in the school yard, it would have been child's play. It was only the sheer brick wall stretching down to the pavement, the cars and buses moving like toys so far below and the blast of the wind against his face that made it terrifying. Don't think about it. Do it.

Alex lowered himself on to the ledge outside Crawley's office. His hands were behind him, clutching on to the window-sill. He took a deep breath. And jumped.

A camera located in an office across the road caught Alex as he launched himself into space. Two floors above, Alan Blunt was sitting in front of the screen. He chuckled. It was a humourless sound. "I told you," he said. "The boy's extraordinary."

Extract 2

From Chapter 7

"I love to kill fish," Sayle went on. "But when I saw this specimen of *Physalia physalis,* I knew I had to capture it and keep it. You see, it reminds me of myself."

"It's ninety-nine per cent water. It has no brain, no guts and no anus." Alex had dredged up the facts from somewhere and spoken them before he know what he was doing.

Sayle glanced at him, then turned back to the creature hovering over him in its tank. "It's an outsider," he said. "It drifts on its own, ignored by the other fish. It is silent and yet it demands respect. You see the nematocysts, Mr Lester? The stinging cells? If you were to find yourself wrapped in those, it would be an exquisite death."

"Call me Alex," Alex said.

He'd meant to say Felix, but somehow it had slipped out. It was the most stupid, the most amateurish mistake he could have made. But he had been thrown by the way Sayle had appeared and by the slow, hypnotic dance of the jellyfish.

The grey eyes squirmed. "I thought your name was Felix."

"My friends call me Alex."

"Why?"

SECTION 3

Extract 3

From Chapter 11

He picked up the dry suit. It was too big for him, although it would probably keep out the worst of the chill. But the cold wasn't the only problem. The tunnel might run for ten metres. It might run for a hundred. How could he be sure that Ian Rider hadn't used scuba equipment to swim through? If Alex went down there, into the water, and ran out of breath halfway, he would drown. Pinned underneath the rock in the freezing blackness. He couldn't imagine a worse way to die.

But he had come so far, and according to the map he was nearly there. Alex swore. This was not fun. At that moment he wished he had never heard of Alan Blunt, Sayle Enterprises or the Stormbreaker. But he couldn't go back. If his uncle had done it, so could he. Gritting his teeth, he pulled on the dry suit. It was cold, clammy and uncomfortable. He zipped it up. He hadn't taken off his ordinary clothes and perhaps that helped. The suit was loose in places, but he was sure it would keep the water out.

Moving quickly now, afraid that if he hesitated he would change his mind, Alex approached the water's edge.

Plot, character and setting

Cliffhanging

> **Objective:** Identify features that writers use to provoke readers' reactions.
> **What you need:** Copies of *Stormbreaker*, rectangles of card.

What to do
- Explain to the children the concept of a cliff-hanger, where an episode or chapter of a story ends in such a way that we want to know what happens next.
- Ask the children to look through the chapter endings of *Stormbreaker*, looking for the phrase or sentence in the closing paragraph that raises a question or sets the mood for the following chapters.
- Working in pairs, ask children to compile the five best cliffhangers, writing the final sentence on one of the cards and making a short note about

how they keep us reading. There's a difference between the end of Chapter 11, which makes us want to know where Alex is going, and the end of Chapter 4, which creates a gives a sense of foreboding.
- Once they have itemised five good cliffhangers ask the children to rank them in order – which one is best?

> **Differentiation**
> **For older/more confident children:** Sort cliffhangers by looking at the different jobs they do – rounding off the mini-story of a chapter with a twist or building a sense of suspense about what lies ahead. Can children identify specific jobs done by certain groups of cliffhangers?
> **For younger/less confident children:** Ask the children to identify the events that end their favourite chapters in the book and look at how these make the reader want to keep turning the page.

Map the adventure

> **Objective:** Identify the main points of sections of text.
> **What you need:** Enlarged copies of Photocopiable page 15 (one for each pair), copies of *Stormbreaker*.

What to do
- Only use this activity after children have finished Chapter 12. Ask them to look across the map identifying when and how each location has featured in the story.
- Direct them towards Chapter 7 and ask them to skim the chapter, noting the features that can be seen in the Sayle complex.
- Trace the route and activity that takes place at the end of Chapter 9.
- Ask them to skim Chapter 10 and note the crucial turning point. Ask them to reflect on what role the 'false sign' played in the plot.
- Having read Chapter 11 and retraced the Dozmary Mine incident, ask the children to

annotate an enlarged version of the map on Photocopiable page 15, recalling which hazards Alex faced at various locations. Number these in the order in which they took place.
- Annotate the map to record what the setting was like. What was the atmosphere like in that library or down the mine?

> **Differentiation**
> **For older/more confident children:** As they annotate the map, ask children to add the different hazards that Alex faced and also to think how the setting was essential to that part of the story. The quad bikes needed isolation. The mine needs to be near the sea – think of the tide coming in, etc.
> **For younger/less confident children:** Children can look across the map recalling events from the story without rereading the text. Locations such as the library, Dozmary mine and the runway are particularly memorable.

Plot, character and setting

Character descriptions

> **Objective:** Identify features that writers use to
> provoke readers' reactions.
> **What you need:** Copies of *Stormbreaker*, scissors, glue.

What to do
● Once they have read as far as Chapter 7 ask
the children to list some of the characters they
have encountered in *Stormbreaker* and make short
notes about what each one is like
● Using Photocopiable page 16 initially, provide
the children with only the description column
and ask them to cut this up and read through
each description.
● Without looking at the book, can they think
to whom each description might be referring?
Ask them to think what words particularly led
them to this conclusion.
● Provide copies of the character cards and ask

children to match the character names to the
descriptions.
● They can now check the descriptions in the
book. The characters are all described when first
seen in the story – though Yassen is an odd one,
being first seen in a photo.

> **Differentiation**
> **For older/more confident children:** Once they have
> completed the activity, ask children to reflect on
> how the description matches the character. What
> impression does the reader gather from Herod's suit
> or Mrs Jones' hairstyle?
> **For younger/less confident children:** From the outset
> provide children with copies of both the descriptions
> and the character name cards. Ask them to start with
> four characters they feel are instantly recognisable,
> then add others on.

The mystery

> **Objective:** Use evidence from across a text to explain
> events or ideas.
> **What you need:** Copies of *Stormbreaker*, reporter's
> notebook.

What to do
● Working in pairs, ask children to re-read the
opening chapters as far as the end of Chapter 2.
● Ask them to check through the book, acting
as detectives. They must imagine that they don't
know the rest of the story! Using their notebook
they need to find clues that things are not as they
seem.
● Focus on the first oddity – that Ian Rider
wasn't wearing a seat belt. Ask them to think
what this clue might denote.
● Ask the children to re-read the funeral, where
there is a host of disquieting clues, including
those who attend, the odd word the vicar uses
and Blunt's driver. Ask the children who they
think these people might be – bearing in mind

a first-time reader doesn't yet know who is good
or bad.
● Re-reading Chapter 2, invite the children to list
the various oddities about the car yard and Alex's
other encounters, paying particular attention to
the questions Alex is starting to ask.
● Note what a first-time reader might think is
going on, then match up their ideas to the story
as the following chapters reveal the truth about
Ian Rider and his death.

> **Differentiation**
> **For older/more confident children:** Ask the children
> to evaluate the degree to which different clues lead
> the reader to a conclusion. Comparing the vicar's
> word 'patriotic' with the driver's gun, which one gives
> a clearer picture?
> **For younger/less confident children:** Recalling the
> events of the opening two chapters, ask the children
> to make a list of events that take place and the
> questions they make us ask about the future of Alex.

Plot, character and setting

Micro-sequences

Objective: Understand how writers use different structures to create coherence and impact.
What you need: Copies of *Stormbreaker*, small pieces of paper or card about 5cm x 8cm.

What to do
● Explain to the children that action sequences in films and stories tend to be made of a series of small stunts and actions. Ask the children if they can think of examples from popular heroic films.
● Ask the children to work in fours and to think of an extended exciting event within *Stormbreaker*. Examples could include the scene in the junk yard once the crusher has started, the parachute jump with the SAS, the quad bike chase, the freezing underground swim, the pursuit of the aeroplane or the final scene over and in the Science Museum.

● Once they have chosen their event, ask the children to use small cards to plot this out over five separate, smaller events. If, for example, they have chosen the chase for the plane, one rectangle could say 'Alex hits the guard with a harpoon gun'. Then a separate one would read 'Alex drives a jeep after the plane'

Differentiation
For older/more confident children: Children can revisit their sequence and see if one of the mini-events on one of their cards could be further divided into two – for example, there are two distinct stages to the harpoon gun tussle with the guard.
For younger/less confident children: Reduce the number of cards children have to complete to three, leading them to separate the event into a simple beginning, middle and end.

Alex and…

Objective: Empathise with characters.
What you need: Pencil, paper.

What to do
● Ask the children to work in pairs. They need to begin by making a list of the various characters with which Alex has an encounter during *Stormbreaker*. Ask them to vary the list, including those who are on his side, such as Blunt, and enemies, such as Sayle.
● Once they have written their list ask children to think through the names, making notes on how each character perceives Alex and what, in turn, Alex makes of them. The way to do this is for each child to take on one of the two roles. If, for example, they are working on Blunt one of them takes on the 'Alex' role while the other plays his boss.

● Once they are in role ask the children to say aloud what they think their character makes of the other one and write short notes about this.
● Can they find any common themes in the relationships? Is there a common sense of suspicion? Are all the villains the same? Who does Alex like? Who likes him? Does Yassen like him?

Differentiation
For older/more confident children: Ask the children to write short sentences that highlight complexities within these relationships. Much as he hates Yassen, is there a certain respect? Blunt is on Alex's side, but are they friends?
For younger/less confident children: Children could purely focus on what Alex makes of each of the characters on the list, writing his responses alongside the names. For each response it may be worth asking if they can think of a portion of the story that supports this view.

Plot, character and setting

Problem and solution

> **Objective:** Use evidence from across a text to explain events or ideas.
> **What you need:** Photocopiable page 17, glue, paper.

What to do
● Think of adventure stories where the hero does incredible things to escape danger.
● Ask the children to think through and list some of the problems Alex faces over the course of the story.
● Look at Photocopiable page 17. Explain to the children that these are some of the problems Alex faces and the solutions he finds to them.
● Warn them that there are some examples of three-stage problem-and-solution sequences, where something extra has to be done to save Alex from danger.
● Ask the children to cut out the problems and solutions and match one to the other, rebuilding them and sticking them down on their paper.

> **Differentiation**
> **For older/more confident children:** Ask the children to think of other ways in which the same problem could have been solved. Is there some gadget that could have been given at the start that would have helped?
> **For younger/less confident children:** This can be done as a sorting activity, separating the texts that read like problems from the texts that read like solutions.

Ian has been here before

> **Objective:** Understand underlying themes in a text.
> **What you need:** Photocopiable page 18.

What to do
● Ask the children to think through the different ways in which Ian Rider is mentioned in *Stormbreaker*. Point out that one theme of the story is the way in which Alex is completing a mission originally undertaken by Ian.
● Ask the children to read through the pointers, on Photocopiable page 18, to the ways in which Ian Rider set Alex up to be able to tackle the tasks he faces.
● As an additional strand to this activity, ask the children if they can rebuild the tracks Ian Rider followed, including what he did, where he went and what happened as he returned to London.
● Read the passage at the start of Chapter 6 where Blunt talks about how Ian prepared Alex. Ask the children to say in what ways they feel Ian's presence can be felt throughout *Stormbreaker*.

> **Differentiation**
> **For older/more confident children:** Ask the children to consider whether Ian should have prepared Alex for a life of danger. Was this out of a sense of duty?
> **For younger/less confident children:** Ask the children to focus on Chapter 11 and the three of the five events listed on Photocopiable page 18 that take place within this chapter.

Map the adventure

Annotate this map showing what happened where...

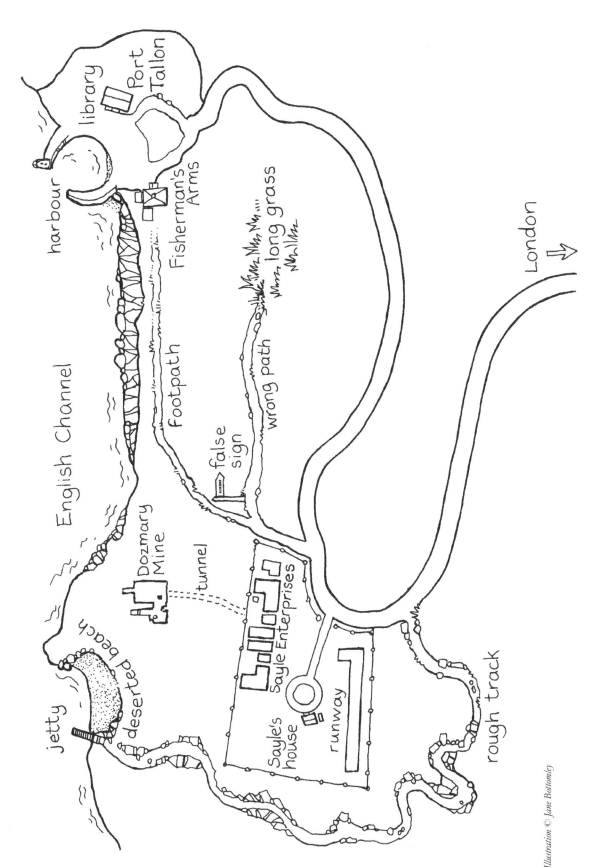

library

Port Tallon

harbour

Fisherman's Arms

long grass

English Channel

Footpath

wrong path

London

false sign

Dozmary Mine

tunnel

Sayle Enterprises

jetty

deserted beach

Sayle's house

runway

rough track

Illustration © Jane Bottomley

Character descriptions

Which character matches the description?

• fourteen, • athletic body • fair hair, cut short	HEROD SAYLE
• late twenties • red hair • round, boyish face	MRS JONES
• grey suit, grey hair, grey eyes • expressionless face • square spectacles	ALEX
• a strange potato-shaped head • black hair	YASSIN GREGOROVICH
• white t-shirt and jeans • late twenties • blond, close-cropped hair • a smooth face	JACK
• expensive black suit • gold signet ring • brightly polished black shoes	BLUNT

Problem and solution

Match the problems Alex faces with their solutions.
Be careful, some solutions are in two stages.

jumping from a ledge outside a window on the fifteenth floor	grab a parachute and jump out, only to find he flies after you	set off your smoke bomb Game Boy inside the plane
being caught sneaking around Sayle Enterprises	lure a rider towards a fence then dive out of the way	use zit cream to smash open the tank
mistakenly saying your real name	pretend you're looking for the toilet	grabbing hold of the flag and gripping on, dangling in mid air
being chased by two riders on 4 x 4 quad bikes	pretend you're nicknamed after a famous football manager	use the abandoned wet suit
swimming through the underwater tunnel	reaching for a flagpole and missing it	use the abandoned quad to go after the other one
landing in a giant tank with a deadly, giant jellyfish	find yourself in a plane with Mr Grin	

Plot, character and setting

Ian has been here before

How did Ian's actions below help Alex in his quest?

A clue left in the bedroom (Chapter 8)	

Ian's visit to Port Tallon Library (Chapter 11)	

The trapdoor at Dozmary mine (Chapter 11)	

Faced with a freezing, underwater tunnel (Chapter 11)	

The grille between the tunnel and laboratory (Chapter 12)	

Talk about it

Interrogation

> **Objective:** Use different question types.
> **What you need:** Copies of *Stormbreaker*.

What to do
- Remind the children that being a spy involves learning and remembering chunks of information. If caught, they need to keep their cool and answer lots of questions under interrogation – and that's what this activity is about.
- Ask the children to work in pairs. They should select and read two consecutive chapters of the book and formulate some questions about it. Ask them to include a mixture of question types, for example: A closed question 'What is the name of the bank manager in Chapter 3?'; an open question 'How do you think Alex was feeling when?'; a leading question 'Do you think that Alex felt afraid when...?'

- Once they have devised their list of questions a pair of children can set a challenge to another member of the class – to read and take in two chapters to such a degree that they can answer quick-fire questions on it.
- Let the challenge begin! The reader must face quick-fire interrogation, keep their cool and try to answer as many questions as they can about the facts of *Stormbreaker*.

> **Differentiation**
> **For older/more confident children:** Turn the activity into a challenge by setting a time limit on the question period – how many questions can they answer in three minutes?
> **For younger/less confident children:** The task can be reduced to one chapter or even a limited number of pages.

Script it

> **Objective:** Perform a scripted scene using dramatic conventions.
> **What you need:** copies of *Stormbreaker*.

What to do
- Once they have read as far as Chapter 11, ask the children to think through the various conversations that have taken place throughout the book. Ask them to pick one they would like to work on. Examples can include Blunt's meeting with Alex, or Alex's meeting with Sayle.
- Ask the children to read through one of these conversations and turn it into a script. This can include lines from the book as well as ones of their own devising.
- Remind the children to include stage directions

that indicate how characters should move and the tone in which lines should be said.
- Ask the children to write out a short, two- or three-minute scripted section of conversation, just like screenwriters.
- Once they have written their script, children could involve other children in acting out the scene.

> **Differentiation**
> **For older/confident able children:** Ask the children to adapt the scene, putting in a few lines that bring out emotions such as tension or anger.
> **For younger/less confident children:** Make the activity a guided writing task: children should prepare their script and act it out.

Talk about it

Motifs

> **Objective:** Plan and manage a group task.
> **What you need:** Photocopiable page 22.

What to do
● Ask the children to think through various action films they have seen and one of the features they have in common with each other – the last minute escape, the big finale, etc.
● Explain that motifs are features that are common to a certain type of story, like the last minute escape in an action story.
● Working in groups of four, ask the children to cut out the rectangles on Photocopiable page 22. Placing them face down, ask the children to take turns to select a motif.

● As a group, ask them to discuss the way that motifs feature both in *Stormbreaker* and in other adventure stories they have encountered. Can they think of how the examples work in *Stormbreaker* and how the motif contributes to the story? They can also write key words in each box as reminders.

> **Differentiation**
> **For older/more confident children:** Ask the children to reflect on the motif, considering why these need to happen in such stories. Why, for example, does it save time for the villain to reveal his plan?
> **For younger/less confident children:** Ask the children to find examples in *Stormbreaker* of a chosen few of the motifs.

The view

> **Objective:** Explore how different texts appeal to readers using varied sentence structures and descriptive language.
> **What you need:** Photocopiable page 23, preferably enlarged to A3.

What to do
● Ask the children to get into groups of four and read through the lines on Photocopiable page 23. Explain that these are 'choice lines' from the text – some of the best lines in the book.
● Explain to the children that they are going to work in 'buzz groups' – small groups that engage in five-minute conversations and build up ideas from these small discussions. Once you have presented the idea, work through the discussion points below, giving children time after each one to read through the text and hold a short discussion. When it feels as if this is falling quiet – move on.
● Ask the children to consider what insights the lines give us into the characters in the story. Characters can be effectively defined by what they say, or, in sentences describing Alex's thoughts, we get an insight into the inner conversation of a character. What insight do the lines give into the feelings of characters? Ask the children to look out for tensions between characters in these lines. Where are the characters disagreeing with each other and where is one character making a sharp comment to another?
● How do the lines contribute to the plot of the story? Look out for ways in which they raise questions or deal with things up ahead, possibly presenting a warning or raising a dilemma.
● How do we respond as readers to these lines? What do we feel as we are reading them? Some of these sentences use good imagery, such as 'skin crawling' and 'dead meat'. Ask the children to look out for examples of imagery and discuss how it works.

> **Differentiation**
> **For older/more confident children:** Ask the children to devise their own two discussion points, centred on the lines on this photocopiable.
> **For younger/less confident children:** Pare down the discussion to a smaller number of lines. Given that the lines are in the order they appear in the story, using the first half means a group can focus on that section of the story.

Talk about it

Violence

> **Objective:** Present a spoken argument.
> **What you need:** Copies of *Stormbreaker*.

What to do

● On the board, write the heading 'Should Alex have a gun?'

● Ask the children to discuss reasons why the author and publisher of this book may have agreed that Alex shouldn't have a gun. Then invite them to consider the other side of the argument. For example, does the the fact that Alex doesn't have a gun impede the story?

● Look at the cover of the book. What is Alex holding instead of a gun? Does the torch look like a gun? Why do they think the publisher has used this image? Is it difficult to make the book look exciting without a hint of violence?

● Read page 205 where Alex encounters the guard while using a harpoon gun. What insights does this give us into the issue of violence in the stories?

● Read page 216. Alex has no gun – but he's a killer. Is the crashing of Mr Grin somehow different?

> **Differentiation**
> **For older/more confident children:** Ask children to draw up a discussion text giving the two sides of an argument for and against arming the character of a boy agent.
> **For younger/less confident children:** Focus straight on the character's thoughts on page 205 and ask them to think through what Alex means when he refuses to kill the guard.

Clues

> **Objective:** Identify the main points of sections of text.
> **What you need:** Photocopiable page 24, copies of *Stormbreaker*.

What to do

● This activity involves two extracts from the book; it can either be undertaken after reading one or once both have been read.

● Ask the children to skim through the chapters shown on Photocopiable page 24 to refresh their memories of the story.

● Looking at the notebook of questions on Photocopiable page 24, ask the children to act as Alex Rider agents, considering and discussing the questions attached to the sets of chapters.

● As they engage in discussion, encourage the children to keep reading the chapters to support their thoughts. Direct them back to passages such as Alex's thoughts about murdering bank managers in Chapter 2, the insights that the snooker game gives us into Sayle's character or the incident when the box is dropped in the same chapter. Once they have had a discussion in their trios, ask the children to join together into a larger or whole-class group and hold a debriefing on their response to the clues.

> **Differentiation**
> **For older/more confident children:** Ask the children to make some hypotheses about what is going on in the story and, for each one, they must come up with some supporting page numbers referencing the text.
> **For younger/less confident children:** Home in on one of the two notebook pages and ask the children to consider the puzzles it raises from the story.

Talk about it

Motifs

Here are some common features of secret agent stories. How do they feature in *Stormbreaker*?

✂

The hero is somehow forced to participate in the adventure	The hero uses fantastic gadgets	The hero has to prove himself to be up to challenges
The hero disobeys superiors	The hero suddenly realises something	The villain reveals his plan
An elaborate death is planned for the hero	The hero reveals a skill nobody knew he had	The hero causes chaos

Talk about it

Choice lines

What do these lines from *Stormbreaker* add to the action, or the feelings or responses of the reader?

- **When Alex meets Blunt**

Alex shivered. There was something about the new arrival that made his skin crawl.

- **When Alex is forced to work for Blunt**

He glanced at the slices of cold lamb on his plate. Dead meat. Suddenly he knew how it felt.

- **When Mrs Jones warns Alex about Yassen**

"Just remember, Alex Rider, you're never too young to die."

- **When, Alex finds a clue from Ian Rider in his room**

Sleep took a long time coming to the dead man's bed.

- **During the quad bike chase**

Whoever these people were, they had tried to run him down, cut him in half and incinerate him. He had to find a way out before they got really serious.

- **When Alex confronts Sayle**

"I'm sorry you were bullied at school," he said. "But lots of kids get bullied and they don't turn into nutcases."

- **When Alex has the chance to shoot a guard**

Whatever Alan Blunt and MI6 wanted to turn him into, he wasn't ready to shoot in cold blood. Not for his country. Not even to save his own life.

Talk about it

Clues

Follow the clues to solve the mysteries of *Stormbreaker*.

Chapter 1
- Why are all these strange people turning up for the funeral?

Chapter 2
- What is the mystery surrounding Ian Rider's car?

Chapter 3
- What is really going on at the 'Royal & General'?

Chapter 7
- What sort of a person is Herod Sayle?

Chapter 8
- What is the mysterious square of paper all about?

Chapter 9
- Why did the submarine make a secret visit?

Illustration © Jane Bottomley

Get writing

Step-by-step danger

> **Objective:** Vary pace through the portrayal of action and selection of detail.
> **What you need:** Small rectangles of paper.

What to do
● Working in pairs, ask the children to think of a dangerous situation, such as climbing a cliff, running along the roof of a moving train or gripping to the runner of a rising helicopter
● Once they have chosen their dangerous scenario, ask the children to take six of the small rectangles of paper and plan step-by-step stages in the danger. Stress that this is partially about the chronology of the event but mainly about smaller dangers within the overall event. For example, a foot that slips while climbing a cliff, or an attack of angry seagulls. If the character slips will there be something to grab on the way down?

● Children who are struggling with ideas may want to consider the involvement of an opponent. What if a character were pursued in their cliff climb, or if the helicopter door were opened by an enemy?
● Another way to spice up the danger is to involve the use of a gadget. What could be built into that watch or shoe heel that could help along the way?

> **Differentiation**
> **For older/more confident children:** Once they have planned six stages children can extend this to add other stages to the danger. If, for example, the falling character clutched a branch, could it begin to snap?
> **For younger/less confident children:** Reduce the number of stages to three and then add another if children are up to it. Once the three are down they can often act as a focus for devising the fourth.

Secret agent story

> **Objective:** Develop and refine ideas in writing.
> **What you need:** Photocopiable page 28.

What to do
● Ask children to think through and list various spy and secret agent stories they have read or seen, focussing on the questions: 'What do these stories have in common?' and 'What works well in these stories?'
● Make a note of children's comments and feed in some ideas such as very nasty villains and breathtaking dangers.
● Ask the children to look through Photocopiable page 28 with a view towards planning their own ideas for a secret agent story.
● Children will need to plan out the characteristics of the agent and villain. Make it clear that either can be male or female.
● There is space to plan a confrontation between agent and villain. Point out that villains often have

an initial, frosty squaring up to their nemesis – as with the snooker game in *Stormbreaker*.
● The last box, 'Is there a personal link for the agent?' raises the fact that in many stories our agent is somehow personally involved in the matters they tackle – in *Stormbreaker*, Alex is pursuing the people who killed his uncle.
● Once they have completed the photocopiable page ask the children to plan out the story they have developed.

> **Differentiation**
> **For older/more confident children:** Other planning details can include looking at how the agent can, in some way, be involved in the outcome – saving someone they care for or clearing themselves from suspicion of crime.
> **For younger/less confident children:** Ask children to select three of the areas to focus on for planning, then include one or two others if they manage to complete this.

Get writing

Agents in your area

> **Objective:** Use settings to engage the reader's interest.
> **What you need:** Paper, pencil, map of the local area.

What to do

- Ask the children to look at the map of the local area, noting various locations with which they are familiar.
- Review sections from the book (for example in Chapters 1 and 2) where Anthony Horowitz has used real London locations.
- Explain to the children that they are going to use their own locality, as seen on the map, as a setting for a secret agent story. To do this they will need to think of what places could serve as the home of the hero or heroine and a secret base for goodies.
- Ask the children to think of other things that could be hidden in the local area. If, for example, the villain is hunting a store of hidden treasure where could this be stashed?
- Looking at their locality ask the children to imagine a chase sequence that could take place across the area, possibly involving entering and leaving buildings. What if the villains were to chase a young hero, starting from the classroom in which they now sit? They might also want to decide where their villain could undertake a dastardly deed from which the heroine or hero could have a narrow escape.
- Ask the children to draw a rough map of the area noting features that could appear in their own secret agent story and how they fit with the overall story line.

> **Differentiation**
> **For older/more confident children:** Encourage the children to add extra detail about colour to each item on their list.
> **For younger/less confident children:** Ask the children to compile a list of the main streets and places before drawing their map.

Dangers

> **Objective:** Use different narrative techniques to entertain and engage the reader.
> **What you need:** Photocopiable page 29.

What to do

- Re-read the scene in Chapter 14 where Alex encounters the jellyfish.
- Ask the children to think through some of the dangers they have known secret agents encounter in books or films and the ways in which they have tackled these problems.
- Ask the children to read through the hazards on Photocopiable page 29. Explain that the idea is that they should imagine themselves as the secret agent who has to face up to these challenges. What would the danger be like? How would it begin?
- Ask the children to write short notes in the boxes alongside each danger, showing how they would tackle it. Point out that the two common ways are to escape it – to get away from the problem – or to overcome it. So it's one thing to find a way out of the flooding cellar, another to locate and pull the plug.
- Allow time for children to research their problem – finding out how helicopters move or looking at images of mansion houses to study the roofs. Such research can throw up useful facts, such as the information that crocodiles can run fast in straight lines but, if you zigzag, they have trouble keeping up.

> **Differentiation**
> **For older/more confident children:** Children could devise means of escape that are specifically focussed on the nature of the danger. How could their agent exploit the weakness of each danger?
> **For younger/less confident children:** Focus the children's thoughts initially on how the danger emerges, how it is heard or seen coming and how it makes its full appearance.

Get writing

The toys

> **Objective:** Develop and refine ideas in writing.
> **What you need:** Small sheets of lined and blank paper of varied sizes, a large sheet of sugar paper, catalogues.

What to do
● Re-read Chapter 6, homing in on the different gadgets noting what they look like and what they do.
● Ask the children to work in groups of four or five. Explain that they are going to devise their own set of secret agent equipment.
● To begin with, ask the children to list the sort of jobs they would like equipment to do. Move them beyond the often immediate desire for gadgets that shoot people, raising the potential for gadgets that climb, track, hide or communicate.
● Once they have some thoughts about the jobs the equipment will do, ask them to flick through catalogues seeking out items that could

be disguised as agents' gadgets. These can range from traditional watches to more up-to-date game and media items.
● Ask the children to divide the gadgets amongst the group with each child writing a report text about their particular item. They can share ideas across the group. As the report texts are completed, add these to the large sheet of sugar paper, building up in poster format the overall secret agent kit.

> **Differentiation**
> **For older/more confident children:** Gadgets are actually features of a story's plot. If they are introduced, they will be used. Ask the children to make short notes as to how each gadget could feature in the story they have been planning.
> **For younger/less confident children:** Children can begin with the initial object – such as a clock – and be asked to think through the ways in which this could be a disguised gadget.

The view

> **Objective:** Establish and balance viewpoints.
> **What you need:** Photocopiable page 30, extract 1.

What to do
● Re-read Extract 1 and ask the children to consider other choices Alex faces throughout *Stormbreaker*. What does he decide to do in each case and what would have happened if he had done something differently?
● Using the tables on Photocopiable page 30 ask the children to plan out short discussion texts, weighing up the pros and cons of the choices shown. Stress that they are to do this as if they were with Alex before he takes his decision – so they do *not* know the outcome.
● Remind the children that, as they think through the two columns in each table, they need to consider the consequences of Alex's actions for

himself. Although he survives, each one had the potential to go the other way and children should factor this into their considerations
● Ask them to consider also the consequences for Alex's mission and the country. Not going through that tunnel would mean not knowing what Sayle was up to – and if Alex hadn't found out...

> **Differentiation**
> **For older/more confident children:** Ask the children to use their ideas on the photocopiable page to write a first-person description of Grandma.
> **For younger/less confident children:** Blank out two of the shapes from the photocopiable page, for example, leaving only the speech bubble and the thought bubble.

Secret agent story

Use this planner to create your own secret agent story.

What is the heroine/hero agent like?	What is the villain like?	What does the villain want?

How did the agent confront the villain?	What dangers will our agent encounter?

How did the agent get into this?	Is there a personal link for the agent?

Get writing

Dangers

How would your secret agent face dangers like these? Make notes overleaf for each one.

1. You are on a high rope bridge and it starts to fray.

2. You end up on the sloping roof of a very tall mansion.

3. You are trapped in a tunnel underground.

4. You find yourself in a room full of spiders.

5. The cave you are trapped in is filling up with water.

6. You end up being chased by hungry crocodiles.

7. You are chased by villains on motorbikes.

8. Someone is after you and they are piloting a helicopter.

Get writing

SECTION

6

The View

Weigh up Alex's decisions during *Stormbreaker*.

Work for Blunt	Don't work for Blunt
_____	_____
_____	_____
_____	_____
_____	_____

Hide in the lorry	Don't hide in the lorry
_____	_____
_____	_____
_____	_____
_____	_____

Go through the flooded tunnel	Don't go through the flooded tunnel
_____	_____
_____	_____
_____	_____

Chase after the plane	Don't chase after the plane
_____	_____
_____	_____
_____	_____

READ & RESPOND: Activities based on *Stormbreaker*

Assessment

Assessment advice

Stormbreaker provides a story from which teachers can gain an insight into children's grasp of how plot and character work together to create a fast-moving story.

As they work through the book, ask the children to note the arc that forms over the whole story – the big uncovering of Herod Sayle's plot, but also the smaller mysteries that are unpicked within the storyline. These take the form of questions that get answered. Who are Ian's mysterious employers? Is Herod Sayle a villain? Where is Yassen?
Make sure children are clear about this question-and-answer structure.

Adventure stories like *Stormbreaker* are always event-driven. As they work through the book, focus on children's understanding of what is happening in each event and how it connects to the wider storyline. Why that long ramble through SAS training? How does the danger in the long grass fit in with Alex's journey to Port Tallon? And why is that journey so important?

In the opening chapters of the story note the degree to which children can make sense of the way Alex's suspicions are aroused. What is so strange about that funeral? Check the extent to which children can peg Alex's actions to the questions he asks. He jumps around 70 metres above London because he wants to know who his uncle was really working for.

Once they reach the chapters set at Port Tallon, assess the way children can interpret information about characters as another means of gaining insight into what is really going on in this operation. One focus here should be the character of Sayle. On the surface he is a philanthropist – so how does the story penetrate the surface? In what ways does it emerge that Sayle is really up to no good?

Chapters

> **Objective:** To understand the significance of events in a story.
> **What you need:** Photocopiable page 32, scissors, glue.

What to do
● This photocopiable picks up on the assessment focus on children's understanding of the significance of, and connection between, events in a story.
● Ask the children to read through the list of chapter titles on Photocopiable page 32. What clues do these offer to the events that took place in them? Only hear a couple of examples.
● Ask the children to work individually, reading the titles, cutting them out and putting them in order.
● Once they have done this ask them to check with a partner – but not to alter their order of events – and note any differences in the order in which they have placed their chapters.
● Discuss with children the order in which they put their chapters and why they did this, listening out for their awareness of the order of events in the story and ways in which they understood that one event led to another.

Chapters

Cut these chapter titles out and place them in the order in which they feature in *Stormbreaker*.

Royal & General	Behind the Door
Double O Nothing	The School Bully
Twelve O'Clock	Death in the Long Grass
Funeral Voices	"So What Do You Say?"
Dozmary Mine	Looking for Trouble